IN THE BEGINNING WAS

RASTAFARIANISM:

RELIGION AND

SPIRITUALITY

OF

RASTAFARI

BY
PROFESSOR NIGEL
JOHNSON

TABLE OF CONTENTS

INTRODUCTION --------------------------------6

CHAPTER 1------------------------------------10

HISTORY OF RASTAFARI IN

JAMAICA------------------------------------10

   Background of Rastafarianism------10

   Modern Rastafarianism----------------13

CHAPTER 2------------------------------------16

WAYS AND STYLES OF LIVING.---16

   Guidance of Life-----------------------17

   Religious/Ritual Practice-------------19

   The Journey of Life (life cycle)------22

   Holy Days and Celebrations(life

cycle)--24

CHAPTER 3------------------------------------26

FAITH--26

   Symbol of Faith-----------------------26

   Prayer and Meditation----------------29

   Expression and Worship--------------32

Art, Music, Drama and Creativity---34

CHAPTER 4------------------------------------38

IDENTITY AND DIVERSITY---------38

Religious Identity----------------------38

Family and Community--------------39

Diversity within the tradition--------43

Attitudes to Other Religions and

Interfaith activities---------------------45

CHAPTER 5------------------------------48

MEANING AND PURPOSE-----------48

Answers to Ultimate Questions------48

CHAPTER 6------------------------------52

VALUES AND COMMITMENT-------52

Moral Issues----------------------------52

Ethical Guidelines---------------------52

Individual Responsibility------------54

Global Vision--------------------------56

WEBSITES ------------------------------58

BIBLIOGRAPHY ------------------------60

INTRODUCTION

Rastafarianism is a religious movement that originated in the black slums of Jamaica. It adopted the ideas of Marcus Garvey, a black nationalist who was born in Jamaica, and employs handpicked passages from the Old Testament by Christians to support its beliefs and rituals.

Religion according to the Oxford dictionary is defined as "Action or conduct indicating belief in, obedience to, and reverence for a god, gods, or similar superhuman power; the performance of religious rites or observances"
The Rastafarian religion is as spiritual as other religions Even though it combines of protestant Christianity, mysticism, and a pan-African political consciousness.

Rastafarians, as the movement's adherents are known, have a unique perspective on their past, present, and future. They "overunderstand" (instead of understanding) people of African heritage in the Americas and elsewhere as "exiles in Babylon" by drawing on Old Testament themes, particularly the Exodus story. They think that the presence of slavery, economic injustice, and racial "downpression" is God's way of testing them (rather than oppression). Rastafarians anticipate their release from captivity and return to Zion, the biblically inspired term for Africa, by turning to the New Testament book of Revelation. Repatriation is one of the objectives of the organization; Ethiopia, the location of a dynastic authority, is the ultimate home of all Africans and the seat of Jah. The Ethiopian emperor, His Imperial Majesty

Haile Selassie I, who was crowned in 1930, is seen by many (though not all) Rastas as the Second Coming of Christ, who has come to save all Black people. Ras Tafari, the emperor's pre - coronation name, serves as the inspiration for the movement's name. Rastafarians from Jamaica are descended from African slaves who were converted to Christianity in that country using the King James Version of the Bible by missionaries. Since English slave owners encouraged false Bible interpretations in order to better manage their slaves, Rastas contend that the King James Version is a corrupted representation of the authentic word of God. Following the crowning of Ethiopian Emperor Haile Selassie I in 1930, Rastafarianism gained ground in Jamaica as a result of the spread of Ethiopianism and Pan-Africanism. A spiritual movement centered on preachers like Leonard Howell, who established the first well-known Rastafarian community in 1940, its adherents gathered around the idea that Selassie was divine. By the 1950s, other branches had emerged, and by the 1980s, Bob Marley's music, a devout Rastafarian, had brought the movement to the attention of the world. Rastafarianism still has adherents in the US, England, Africa, and the Caribbean despite the loss of its most significant individuals in the deaths of Selassie in 1975 and Marley in 1981

Christianity in Jamaica by missionaries using the text of the King James Version of the Bible. Rastas maintain that the King James Version may be a corrupted account of the true word of God, since English slave owners promoted incorrect readings of the Bible so as to better control slaves. Rastas believe that they will come to know the true meanings of biblical scriptures by cultivating a mystical consciousness of oneself with Jah, called "I-and-I." Rastas read the Bible selectively, however, emphasizing passages from Leviticus that admonish the cutting of hair and beard and therefore the eating of certain foods and that prescribe rituals of prayer and meditation. supported their reading of the Old Testament, many Rasta men uphold patriarchal values, and therefore the movement is often charged with sexism by both insiders and outsiders. "Iyaric," or "Dread-talk," is that the linguistic style of many Rastas, who substitute the sound of "I" surely syllables.Rastafari "livity," or the principle of balanced lifestyle, includes the wearing of long hair locked in its natural, uncombed state, dressing within the colours of red, green, gold, and black (which symbolize the vital force of blood, herbs, royalty, and Africanness), and eating an "I-tal" (natural, vegetarian) diet. Religious rituals include prayer services, the smoking of ganja (marijuana) to realize better "itation" (meditation) with Jah, and "bingis" (all-night drumming ceremonies). Reggae music grew out of the Rastafari movement and was made popular throughout the planet by the Jamaican singer and songwriter Bob Marley..

CHAPTER 1

HISTORY OF RASTAFARI IN JAIMACA

BACKGROUND OF RASTAFARIANISM

The roots of Rastafarianism are often traced to the 18th century, when Ethiopianism and other movements that emphasized an idealized Africa began to require hold among black slaves in the Americas. For those that had been converted to Christianity, the Bible offered hope through such passages as Psalm 68:31, foretelling of how "Princes shall begin of

Egypt and Ethiopia shall soon stretch out her hands unto God."

The ethos was strengthened through the late 19th century rise of the fashionable Pan-African movement and particularly the teachings of Jamaican-born Marcus Garvey, who reportedly told his followers to "Look to Africa where a black king shall be crowned, he shall be the Redeemer." Additionally, the 1920s brought such influential proto-Rastafarian texts as "The Holy Piby" and "The Royal Parchment Scroll of Black Supremacy to Jamaica."

HAILE SELASSIE AND THE RISE OF RASTAFARIANISM

On All Souls' Day , 1930, Ras Tafari Makonnen was crowned Emperor Haile

Selassie I of Ethiopia. Believed to be a descendant of King Solomon and therefore the Queen of Sheba, Selassie assumed the titles of King of Kings, Lord of Lords and therefore the Conquering Lion of the Tribe of Judah, to some fulfilling the Biblical prophecy of a black king that had been emphasized by Garvey.

Jamaican preachers began promoting the ruling authority of Selassie over King George V (Jamaica was then a colony of England) and by the mid-1930s the Ethiopian emperor was regarded by followers as the living embodiment of God. Although no formalized central church materialized, the budding factions of Rastafarianism found footing through their belief in a lineage that dated to the ancient Israelites, black superiority and therefore the repatriation of the diaspora from the oppressive land of "Babylon" to Africa. Their movement reflected a variety of influences, including Old Testament instructions on avoiding certain foods and a local belief in the spiritual powers of marijuana. Preachers like Robert Hinds, Joseph Hibbert and Archibald Dunkley achieved prominence within the decade, but to several scholars the most important figure in early Rastafarianism was Leonard Howell. A former member of Garvey's Universal Negro Improvement Association, Howell attracted an outsized following after returning from extensive travels to Jamaica in 1932, and outlined the nascent movement's principles with the publication of "The Promise Key" circa 1935. Although a replacement chapter of Jamaican history commenced with its formal independence from England in 1962, lingering negative attitudes and governmental oppression of Rastafari remained. the foremost notorious incident occurred on what became known as "Bad Friday" in April 1963, when police arrested and beat an estimated 150 innocent Rastafarians in response to a militant flare-up at a gasoline station. A visit by Emperor Selassie in April 1966 appeared to foster an improved perception among non-believers, though there have been still ugly moments, like the Rastafarian involvement in the 1968 riots over a ban of professor and activist Walter Rodney. By the first 1970s, it had been clear the movement had become entrenched among the youth of Jamaica. This was underscored by the successful 1972 presidential campaign of People's National Party leader Michael Manley, who carried a "rod of correction" gifted to him by Emperor Selassie and used Rasta dialect at rallies. While Rastafarian practices spread with the migration of Jamaicans to England, Canada and therefore the United States from the 1950s into the 1970s, its worldwide growth was aided by the influence of adherents on popular music genre . An early contributor during this field was Count Ossie, who began drumming at Nyahbinghi spiritual sessions and helped develop the design that became known as ska. Later, the movement found its most vital ambassador in Bob Marley. A convert to Rastafari and founding father of reggae music, the charismatic Marley unabashedly referenced his beliefs in his songs, achieving widespread acclaim within the 1970s through universally appealing themes of brotherhood, oppression and redemption. Marley toured widely, bringing his sound to Europe, Africa and therefore the U.S., while becoming the poster child for Rastafarian causes. Meanwhile, the growing popularity of Rastafarianism among people of differing races and cultures led to changes in a number of its stricter codes. The 1970s book "Dread: the Rastafarians of Jamaica," by Roman Catholic priest and caseworker Joseph Owens, highlighted a number of the challenges facing the movement, with some sects electing to deemphasize the importance of black superiority in favor of a message of equality

\

MODERN RASTAFARIANISM

A turning point for Rastafarianism came in 1975, when Emperor Selassie died and made his followers to confront the contradiction of a living deity passing away. In 1981, the movement lost its second major figure with the death of Marley from cancer. Always a decentralized faith and culture, Rastafari attempted to introduce a unifying element with a series of international conferences within the 1980s and '90s. Smaller divisions, like African Unity, Covenant Rastafari and therefore the Selassian Church, emerged round the turn of the millennium, the identical period which brought the passing of longtime leaders Prince Emanuel Charles Edwards (1994) and the Prophet Gad (2005).

As of 2012, it had been estimated that there were approximately 1 million Rastafarians throughout the world. Its traditions continue in communities within the U.S., England, Africa, Asia and Jamaica, where the govt has co-opted much of its symbolism through efforts to market tourism. Attempting to form amends for past transgressions, the Jamaican government decriminalized marijuana in 2015, and in 2017 Prime Minister Andrew Holness formally apologized to Rastafarians for the Coral Gardens debacle.

CHAPTER 2

WAYS AND STYLES OF LIVING.

There is no formal, central organisation of Rastafari. They avoid bureaucratic or hierarchical organisations, which they see as characterising the social structures of Babylon. They reject governments, especially the colonial British government in Jamaica,
but after this led to 1962 they remained opposed to 'western civilisation' in general. The organisation of Rastafari is individualised, cellular, or reticulate in its structure. there's an open form of Rastafari organisation called a 'house' or 'mansion'.

There is no individual leadership equivalent to a priest among Rastafaris generally, although a number of the more structured houses, like Bobo Shanti and the Nyabinghi Order, do have priests. A 'leading brother' acts as spokesperson during group
meetings. Houses can have a chaplain, an area treasurer, a sergeant at arms, and a recording secretary; or a number of these roles
– or none of them. In Jamaica, Rastafaris often follow a communal way of living, patterned on the first Pinnacle communes, where they grow their own food and ganja. Membership isn't based on baptism but on adoption of Rastafari beliefs and practices. This provides a broad solidarity of mainstream Rastafari, who largely support the three main Rastafari principles of

the divinity of Haile Selassie , the spiritual use of ganja, and therefore the principle of repatriation to Africa. Rastafari are then liberal to live
their lives individualistically without collective discipline. This provides a collective sense of spiritual identity that is not
supported by any specific ritual obligation. Houses strive for collective deciding , reaching a consensus on problems with importance to the group whether or not this requires extensive debate. Rastafari characterise themselves as a 'brotherhood' or
'brethren'. As there's no formal membership; there is a general ethos of coming, going, and participating solely on conviction

GUIDANCE FOR LIFE

Rastafari is more a few way of living than an acceptance of doctrine. An early codification of morality was written as ten principles by the Jamaican Rastafari elder, Sam Brown (1925-1998), who was the primary Rastafari to run for political office:

1. We strongly object to sharp implements utilized in the desecration of the figure of Man; e.g. trimming and shaving, tattooing of the skin, and cutting of the flesh.

2. We are basically vegetarians, making scant use of certain animal flesh, outlawing the use of swine's flesh in any form, shell fishes, scaleless fishes, snails, etc.

3. We worship and observe no other God but Rastafari, outlawing all other kinds of Pagan worship yet respecting all believers.

4. We love and respect the brotherhood of mankind, yet our ex is to the sons of Ham [black people].

5. We disapprove and abhor utterly hate, jealousy, envy, deceit, guile, treachery, etc.

6. We don't comply with the pleasures of present-day society and its modern evils.

7. We are avowed to form a world of one brotherhood.

8. Our duty is to extend the hand of charity to any brother in distress, firstly for he's of the Rastafari order – secondly, to any human, animals, plants, etc.

9. We do adhere to the normal laws of Ethiopia.

10. Thou shall give no thought to the assistance , titles and possession that the enemy in his fear may seek to bestow on you; resolution to your purpose is the love of rastafari.

In general, Rastafari attempt to live in a way that defends the poor and oppressed, a worldview inherited from the first movement.

The White race is seen as oppressive, but not all White race are evil, they accept individual White race on merit unless they are found guilty of racism. Rastafari became less concerned with racial separatism and aggression after the 1960s. There is, however, no uniform view on race. While there's a general principle that Jah is in everyone, Rastafari view themselves as a people apart. for several the sense is that they are a 'covenant people' like the Jews with special responsibilities rather than being a superior race, as early Rastafari preachers claimed. this suggests striving towards the ideal way of life including living off

the land, growing their own food, not using the land for commercial profit, and eating only clean ital food (see 'Ethical Guidelines' below). this is often seen as living in a natural 'African' way. this is often phrased as being a 'conscious' not a 'careless'
Ethiopian (using Ethiopian as a logo for all black people). those that are careless do not follow the Rasta way, the conscious
do, and salvation comes from being a conscious Ethiopian

RELIGIOUS/RITUAL PRACTICE

A ritual celebration is named a 'duty', but there's no obligation to attend. Participation in ritual and ceremony is voluntary. In all types of Rastafari ritual, ganja (a sort of marijuana) is smoked as a sacrament, often called 'wisdom weed' or 'holy herb'. It is used to meditate, called 'head resting with Jah' (see 'Prayer' below). this is often smoked through a glass or wooden chillum pipe

called a 'chalice' or 'cup' because sections of Deuteronomy and other biblical books that mention sending up incense to God

from a chalice or cup are read as pertaining to smoking ganja. Rituals also generally involve chanting, drumming, meditating,

dancing, and prayer. Most Rastafari communities hold weekly and monthly meetings. the foremost important is the Nyabinghi, held

on special occasions for the needs of celebration; more frequent are reasoning sessions. There also are less ritualised weekly meetings called 'business meetings' which are forums to unravel problems and to discuss ongoing programmes such as community projects.

'Reasonings' are "a ceremony of varying degrees of ritual in which participants access the spirit through the ritual smoking of

herb (ganja) and therefore the use of word/sound/power for the purpose of gaining clarity about spiritual, philosophical, political, and

social truth claims" (Christensen 2014: 61). The discussion is cooperative not competitive, with the aim to succeed in consensus

about the implications of a specific insight. there's a democratic atmosphere in which each member is given time for full and free debate on all subjects. Everyone has the prospect to speak for as long as necessary. Participants tell one another about

revelations that they had in dreams and meditation. Reasonings are a sort of ritual discussion that can also include daily prayers,

meditation, drumming, chanting, hymns, lyrics, and poetry. Another name for the sessions is 'groundings'. Monthly meetings begin within the early evening, last the whole night, and involve dancing, smoking and eating. Such meetings often begin with Psalm 122, then a Rastafari prayer, scripture readings, comments, and end with the Rastafari anthem . this is often followed by

drumming and singing for fun for some hours.

Larger celebrations are called Nyabinghi. In Jamaica, members from everywhere the island join celebrations; these are held in various parts of the island, sort of a convention for Rastas. Nyabinghi last for one to 3 days or for a whole week. The word

'Nyabinghi' comes from East Africa , where it denoted a religio-political resistance movement to colonialism from the 1890s to

1928. The term in Jamaica meant "death to the Black and White oppressors" before its association with Rastafari ceremony. It

is a gathering of brethren for inspiration, exhortation, feasting, smoking, and social contact. Nyabinghi is additionally called 'Groundation' or 'Grounation'. the primary one was held in March 1958, called by

Prince Emmanuel Edwards in southern magnolia , Jamaica.
It is the central communal ritual of Rastafari. It originated as a ritual burning down of Babylon. The drumming, dancing, building and tending the hearth were meant to unleash cosmic energy pervading the universe to eliminate the forces of imbalance. While

they can be held spontaneously, they're routinely held on holy days and on days commemorating significant events in

Rastafari history. Anyone can hold a Nyabinghi; first they get the support of their immediate group, then they announce the time

and place for the gathering, then other Rastas arrive early to line up a tabernacle (see 'Places of Worship' below), prepare food, socialise, then the ceremony begins at sunset. Drumming, chanting, dancing, and smoking ganja continues throughout the night and may last for several days. Proper dress for ladies is a long skirt, a top with long sleeves, and a covered head. Women traditionally cannot attend if menstruating.

THE JOURNEY OF LIFE (LIFE CYCLE)

Birth is widely known with a Nyabinghi, the identical can be held for a formal marriage ceremony. However, it's not necessary, and a
man and woman cohabitation are regarded as married whether or not a ceremony is held. there's generally no funeral
ceremony for Rastas, who believe reincarnation and that following Rastafari ways faithfully grants eternal life. Only evil things

die. Atoms form new babies and life continues. People only die if they're unfaithful to Jah and have not followed the ways that

grant proper self-preservation. this suggests that a true Rasta cannot die. When people do die, it's explained away by saying the

dead person had strayed from true path of Rastafari somehow. Death is seen as unnatural and avoidable, an evil caused

by the influences of Babylon. Dying is named 'transitioning' to denote that it is not the end of that person's life but a change to a new body. Rastafari believe reincarnation occurs with the identical identity despite a change in physical form. this is often how the line

of black prophets from Moses to Jesus to Haile Selassie is of the same person. This notion connects the Israelites of the Bible to Africans and Rastas because the chosen people; Rastas and black people generally are the biblical Israelites reincarnated.

However, notable Rasta elders have died after living exemplary lives following Rastafari codes of conduct. This has brought some reckoning of death among Rastafari. the primary Rastafari funeral was for a Nyabinghi elder, Bongo Tawney, the chairperson
of the Nyabinghi Order. it had been conducted and presided over by Nyabinghi priests in Jamaica in April 2010. The Nyabinghi Order
were previously the foremost opposed to funeral rituals, claiming "let the dead bury their dead", implying Rastas should have nothing to try to to with death at all.

HOLY DAYS AND CELEBRATIONS(LIFE CYCLE)

The following holy days are observed by Rastafari:

1. Ethiopian Christmas on 7th January. Ethiopian Christmas is observed on the date of the Orthodox Church celebration of the birth of Jesus, usually on or around the 7th January, using the Julian calendar rather than the Gregorian calendar to calculate the date of his birth. Ethiopian holy days are observed because of their importance to Haile Selassie I, who was an Ethiopian Orthodox Christian.

2. Groundation (or Grounation) Day on 21st April. This is the date when Haile Selassie I visited Jamaica in 1966.

3. Ethiopian Constitution Day on 16th July. The date commemorates the proclamation of the first modern constitution of Ethiopia by Haile Selassie I

4. Birthday of Emperor Haile Selassie I on 23rd July

5. Marcus Garvey's Birthday on 17th August.

6. Ethiopian New Year's Day on 11th September. In leap years on the Gregorian calendar this falls on 12th September.

CHAPTER 3

FAITH

Many of the Rastafari stories or mythology surround Haile Selassie . one among the founding myths is that Haile Selassie was descended from the kid of the Queen of Sheba and King Solomon, who successively was descended from the biblical King David.Haile Selassie himself claimed this legendary heritage. it's used to back up the claim that the Rastafari are the Israelites (the people of King David) reborn, and thus God's chosen people. the primary marijuana was grown on the grave of King Solomon,according to another mythological story, connecting this biblical heritage to the plant that Rastafari use as a sacrament. There are stories that, when he visited in 1966, Haile Selassie left a constitution that was kept hidden by the government of Jamaica,guarded from the people, who are often charged under the authority of this document. The constitution sets out the rights of Rastafaris, which is why the govt chose to hide it, since it undermined their own (in Rastafari eyes, illegitimate) authority.A story that expressed their millenarian hopes is that of the seven-mile flotilla of ships coming to require them to Africa for repatriation

SYMBOL OF FAITH

A central symbol for the Rastafari is the lion. One of Haile Selassie's titles was the 'Conquering Lion of Judah'. Representations of lions can be seen on Rastafari houses, flags, tabernacles, and artworks. The lion represents the 'King of Kings' and the dominant maleness of the movement. The lion is a symbol of strength and vigour. Rastafaris try to embody the spirit of the lion: proud, independent, and strong. The dreadlocks are likened to a lion's mane, and also to the biblical Samson. Rastafaris sometimes call themselves Nazarites, as they follow the Nazarite vow to remain unshaven, found in Numbers 6:5. Being unshaven is seen as natural and unencumbered. Initially it was a symbol of defiance to Jamaican society that saw long hair on men as a symbol of disorder and degeneration; the dreadlocks said that they were outside Jamaican society. Rastafaris called themselves 'dreads', where dread meant power and rebellion. Mid-20th century conservative Jamaican society saw it as unkempt, dirty, and dangerous.

Police and teachers used to cut off Rastas' hair in the 1950s and 1960s. However, following the popularity of reggae music and the spread of Rastafari culture beyond Jamaica, dreadlocks have become a symbol of the Rastafari that presents less of an immediate challenge, having become familiar and to an extent sanitised. Dreadlocks for the Rastafari still symbolise power, with some calling them 'telepathic antennas' (Christensen 2014: 71). Rastafari colours are red, green, gold, and black. Red, black and green were the colours of the Garvey movement. Red signifies the blood of martyrs in Jamaican history from the Maroons to Marcus Garvey. Black is the colour of Africans from whom 98 per cent of Jamaicans have descended. Green stands for the vegetation of Jamaica and signifies hope of victory over oppression. Gold is from the Jamaican flag, a cross over green and black. Rastas consciously created a new type of language, variously called Iyaric, livalect (rather than dialect), I-talk, 'dreadtalk', 'soul language', or 'hallucinogenic language' (see 'Expression and Worship' below). Rastafari viewed English as a colonial imposition of Babylon, but they had lost their original African languages through slavery. Iyaric inverts the English language symbolically, for example 'oppression' becomes 'downpression' because it drags you down. Rastas strive to use language in a way that unites sound, word, and power, so that words that have a negative valence also have a negative sound, and words with a positive valence have a positive sound. Some individual words are given specific meaning in Rastafari language, for example 'Israelite' and 'Ethiopian' mean the same thing, referring to a holy people, chosen by God. They use the symbol of 'the Beast' from the biblical Book of Revelation for Babylon, which means the oppressive colonial, imperial system of which slavery was a part, and more widely everyone who is not Rasta. Babylon is a general symbol for evil and oppression. The image of the African continent is also a frequent part of Rastafari visual iconography, a symbol of the Promised Land.

For some Rastafaris, there's no specific building for worship; they meet for weekly reasoning sessions in believers' home or a community centre. In Jamaica, it's more common for Rastafari to live together in a commune, presided over by an elder, with a central yard for reasoning and Nyabinghi. In some yards there's what is called a tabernacle, which may be constructed for specific ceremonies or are often a permanent feature. The tabernacle may be a space that centres the Nyabinghi and reasonings, which otherwise have a free-flowing structure. Tabernacles have a dirt-floor, a circular bamboo frame and a thatch decorated with Rastafari symbols like the red, gold, and green colours, the lion, and depictions of the continent of Africa. They can also include a fireplace key, a high pile of stones with a wood fire on top, which is employed in the Nyabinghi ceremony. the hearth key man is responsible of the fire at ceremonies. The Nyabinghi Order has an altar at the centre of their tabernacles

PRAYER AND MEDITATION

Chanting, prayer, and meditation are a part of Rastafari ceremonies. Meditation may be a way to be in communion with

Jah, and through which they are available to realise what is true or false in the Bible and what has been omitted in the Babylon translations.

Rastafari meditate through 'head resting with Jah'. it's a way of knowing their inner self, understanding the 'book within' that contains divine revelation. Prayer begins and ends meetings. Prayer and meditation are accompanied with smoking ganja for heightened spiritual sensations. Rastafari enter a deep trance like state after smoking a spliff or chillum pipe. there's a specific prayer that accompanies ganja smoking: "Glory be to the daddy and to the maker of creation As it was in the beginning is now and ever shall be World without

end: Jah Rastafari: Eternal God Selassie I".
there's a specific prayer to Haile
Selassie:

 "So we hail our God, Selassie I, Eternal
God, Ras Tafari, hear us and help us and
cause Thy face to shine upon us, Thy
children" used on a day to day to
petition him. Women cover their hair to
wish.

 The main religious journey for Rastafari
is repatriation, or return to Africa. This
journey seeks to reverse the forced
movement of black slaves from Africa to
Jamaica and other colonies by the ecu
empires. the first Rastafari preachers
spoke of ships coming from Ethiopia to
require them to land specially reserved
for them in Africa by Haile Selassie. it

had been a journey to a land where they hoped to be free from oppression and racism. Repatriation was thought to be imminent within the 1950s. There was even an aborted attempt at repatriation in 1959, where many Rastafari gathered at docks in Jamaica waiting for the ships to arrive to require them away. Then in 1966 the visit by Haile Selassie to Jamaica was interpreted as the last step before repatriation. However, Haile Selassie reportedly encouraged Rastafari elders to support liberation in Jamaica before trying to come to Ethiopia. He did grant around 500 acres in Ethiopia at Shashamane for members of the African diaspora who wished to settle there, reciprocally for their support during the war with Italy. Rastas, particularly , were drawn to Shashamane by this offer. Some Rastafari communities were established on this land, as of 2014 there have been still around 800 Rastafari at Melka Oda near Shashamane, and some in the cities of Addis Ababa and Bahir Dar. However, it became harder for Rastafari in Ethiopia after the deposition of Haile Selassie in 1974, when the Marxist revolutionaries nationalised the land the king had granted them.

Furthermore, there was less enthusiasm for repatriation after the Ethiopian famine within the 1980s. it's still common for Rastafari to visit Ethiopia on pilgrimages without settling permanently. for several Rastafaris in the 21st century, it's not a physical or literal repatriation to Ethiopia but a symbolic one, achieved through connecting and celebrating the African side of their identity.

Repatriation to Africa are often interpreted in both physical and spiritual ways. Spiritual repatriation occurs through becoming fully aware of their African identity, discovering the reality about themselves through 'head resting' with Jah. Fairfield House in Bath has become an area of pilgrimage for Rastas in the UK as it was the home of Haile Selassie during his exile in Bath

(1936-41),and now houses a museum
and gallery.

EXPRESSION AND WORSHIP

Rastafari 'dread-talk' or iyaric may be a
conscious construction of language as a
form of religious and political expression.
it's based on the Jamaican dialect, or
patois, particularly the syntax and
grammar. The syntax is nearly devoid
of subject-object opposition and verbs.
Rastafari use words philosophically. The
pronouns 'me' and 'you' are replaced
with 'I and I'. this is often to try to
overcome binary oppositions and
identify with the sufferers and
oppressed of society. the utilization of

'I' as the first and second person pronoun is a way of reminding each person of their worth and value as not a 'slave by nature'. 'I' is employed as both subject and object. 'I' also replaces the prefixes in certain words, like 'I-ceive' instead of 'receive', 'desire' becomes 'I-sire', and 'create' becomes 'I-rate'. the utilization of 'I' expresses the unity and interconnectedness of all persons as incarnations of Jah. 'I' stands for the power to see. it's a central concept of Rastafari word/sound/power. 'I' is conscious of the connection to Jah, whereas 'me' is unconscious of this. Seeing and knowing are synonymous for the Rastafari. they modify a negative to a positive sound vibration e.g. 'dedicate'

to 'livicate', 'library' to 'truebrary'. they create sound vibrations descriptive, e.g. 'destroy' to 'downstroy' because destruction tears things down. Rastafari ask themselves as kings and queens, and therefore the knitted tams that cover their
dreads are called 'crowns.

Rastafari have a verbal culture centred on philosophising. it's a formulation of language that is used as a way of fostering group identity. 'Reasoning' is that the name given to Rastafari discourse, during which members come together spontaneously on a regular basis to possess lengthy discussions on any subject; people join and leave fluidly, topics change rapidly.

it's how they interpret the world. Rastafari avoid language that contributes to servility, self-degradation, and objectification. they struggle to use language that sounds like what it is, for instance 'down-pression' in place of 'oppression' because it drags you down. Language and music have power for the Rastafari. Chanting the name of Haile Selassie resurrects him. Words have creative force. this concept comes from the African concept of nommo, that words and word-sounds have innate power. Emancipation requires a replacement language to liberate; the language of Babylon enslaves. this is often a process rather than a defined lexicon. it's a way of fighting against oppression and slavery through language, which they deem a spiritual battle, a battle of consciousness expressed through Language.

ART, MUSIC, DRAMA AND CREATIVITY

  Rastafari are very influential for the artistic and cultural works of Jamaica, including literature, poetry, painting, sculpture and carving, ceramics, theatre, dance, and music. Rastafari use art as a medium for social and spiritual messages, not simply decoration. it's a way to transform society. Rasta artists use found materials, like boards, glass, and cardboard, keep with their veneration of nature and identification with the poor. They eschew expensive materials. Their works attempt to portray the daily experience of the poor. Art for the Rastafari is about the enrichment of life not just display. Since the 1970s, Rastafari imagery has become more commercialised because it has been spread alongside reggae music. The cultural impact of Rastafari, especially in Jamaica, has been much greater than the amount of adherents would suggest. Music features a religious purpose, which Rastafari phrase as 'churchical'. Traditional Rastafari music has its roots in 19th century gospel music and African drumming. Chanting and drumming feature heavily in meetings. Three sorts of drum are used: bass, an outsized drum; fundeh, a smaller upright drum; and peta (repeater) a good smaller drum. Count Ossie introduced ritual drumming within the early days of the movement; his rhythms were recorded from 1960. The drums each have a symbolic role: "The downbeat of the drummer symbolises the death of the oppressive society but it's answered by the akette drummers with a lighter upbeat, a resurrection of the society through the facility of Ras Tafari" (Barrett 1977: 193). "The steady pulsing beat of the gran casa provides constant pressure which works to cause the end of an oppressive Western system. The regular one-two heartbeat rhythm of the fundeh grounds and comforts. The repeater allows vent for protest also as an avenue for the creative improvisation of the individual" (Christensen 2014: 66). the thought is to call to Africa through music. it's a music of invocation that aims to invoke the spirit and help it get up over the oppressive system of Babylon. The Rastafari anthem is taken from the anthem of the Garvey movement, "Ethiopia, Land of Our Fathers", and is usually a part of Rastafari ceremonies.

  Rastafari music has had a substantial influence on mainstream music in America and Europe. Rastafari music.

CHAPTER 4

IDENTITY AND DIVERSITY

Understanding how individuals develop a way of identity and belonging through faith or belief;
Exploring the variability , difference and relationships that exist within and between religions, values and beliefs.

RELIGIOUS IDENTITY

Rastafari identities specialise in trying to recreate themselves in their image of Africans. this suggests rejecting ways of living associated with Babylon and adopting those of Rastafari. it's an elite and exclusive identity; they are the chosen people and everyone who doesn't follow their ways is part of Babylon. One must have insight to simply accept the divinity of Haile Selassie.

However, they are doing not have formal organisations or doctrinal orthodoxy which means that how individual Rastafari construct their

identity has fluidity and openness. There are some accepted identifying characteristics. the foremost well-known and immediately recognisable mark of Rastafari identity is that the cultivation of dreadlocks. Rastafari are forbidden to chop their hair, following the Old

Testament law that prohibits trimming and shaving of the hair (the Nazarite vow mentioned above), and also of tattooing. For the Rastafari, dreadlocks are "a sacred and inalienable a part of his identity" (Chevannes 1994: 145). The hair is named a crown, compared to the crown of Emperor Haile Selassie or the mane of a lion. within the early movement, dreadlocks were a challenge to the European colonialist constructions of race that deemed African hairstyles bad and European hairstyles good. they're a celebration and acceptance of Africanness. Rastafari identity is additionally expressed through speech by using 'dreadtalk', a way of speaking that distinguishes Rastafari from non-Rastafari. Some Rastafari study Ethiopian history and therefore the Amharic language.

There also are distinctive Rastafari diet restrictions (see below), the smoking of ganja, and wearing tams over their dreadlocks, which serve to separate

Rastafari from Babylon, which may mean all non-Rastafari. Rastafari know who they're and carry themselves with self-confidence due to this strong sense of identity.

FAMILY AND COMMUNITY

Despite the Rastafari rejection of the ways of Babylon, for much of the movement's history their family structure has reproduced the patriarchal system that also characterised the colonial society of Jamaica. the person was the head of family and the woman was subordinate to him. The husband was called 'king-man'. Women were called 'daughters' or 'sistren' or 'queens'.

There has, however, been historical variation within the roles of women in Rastafari. At first, women were active within the early groups as they were in contemporaneous Revival movements. Then there was a virtual disappearance of girls except as spouses in the 1960s. Women could only be 'grown' into Rastafari by a Rastaman. a lady could only be Rastafari through her 'kingman'.

 Then from the 1970s, women began claiming space for themselves as Rastawomen. Prior to the late 1970s, the status of girls in Rastafari beliefs was as fallen creatures, echoing their status within the OldTestament. There was a strict division of labour, with women within the domestic sphere and men in the public sphere. Women were often excluded from deciding . A wife must obey her husband, cover her hair, and wear what her husband told her to wear. Women were said to seek out their salvation through men. Women for much of the Rastafari movement didn't participate in public reasonings, and infrequently went to celebrations. They didn't have the status of an elder in the house. There was a particular ideology of the subordination of girls among the Rastafari. Attitudes to women were the identical as those in Jamaican society more widely, and located among the British colonisers the Rastafari opposed as Babylon.

However, the status of girls has been changing since the 1970s. Women are coming into the movement independently,
 rather than being brought in by men. they're present at celebrations, participate in chanting and dancing, and not cover their dreadlocks. Women are often the most breadwinners and the main caregivers for children. However, it's often important for men to remain at home with the children and spend lots of time with them. Family life is vital and highly regarded. this is often a way of addressing the family system in slavery, which was disrupted by the control of slave masters, and sometimes meant that men were unable to remain

with their partners and children. Rastafari against this focus on a cohesive family with defined roles. Fathers try to be active and positive role models for children, for instance by cooking meals and nurturing young children. In Jamaica, some men practised polygamy or secret polygamy (where the varied wives were unaware of each other), claiming that it had been a traditional African practice. However, this practice was resisted by women and didn't take hold. Some Rastafari women observe menstrual taboos, mainly not cooking or attending Nyabinghi while menstruating. there's a difference in the length of time among the mansions; 7 days for the Nyabinghi Order, 21 days for Bobo Shanti, whereas others don't have the prohibition.

Rastawomen joining the movement in their title rather than as queens of Rastamen have challenged many of the assumptions and stereotypes of girls . there's a tension between feminism as a liberation ideology and Rastafari as a liberation ideology that also subordinated women. Rastawomanism emerged as Rastafari women's ideology of liberation within Rastafari against structures of racial, class, and sexual subordination. The code became seen as a way of separating the self from Babylon and modelling African regal dress. Women in Rastafari portrayed themselves as 'African Queens' with natural beauty that's not modelled on European standards of beauty. Many claim their right to settle on their own dress. they like the title 'queen' to 'daughter' or 'dawta'. They use the symbol of the lioness who partners the lion. Head wraps became a logo of militancy analogous to dreadlocks instead of a covering that diminished them. Rastawomen smoke ganja openly and attend Nyabinghi, participating fully in reasonings and playing drums.

  Rastafari value community among brethren and are active in community programmes. They represented rock bottom segment of Jamaican social classes within the early years when the movement spread in the slums, which meant that community organising amongst the poor has always been a crucial feature of the movement. However, this sense of community initially was exclusive, as they sought to withdraw from Jamaican society, which they experienced as ruled by whites but built on black labour, while exploiting them and giving them nothing reciprocally . They experienced violence from the Jamaican police and other authorities. This position has changed since the 1970s. Rastafari became more curious about liberating Jamaica, making it the land of the Rastafaris, then they have become more active in Jamaican society rather than withdrawing from it. for instance ,

Rastafari never voted until a Rastafari elder, Ras Sam Brown, first stood for election in 1961 for his Suffering People's Party.

DIVERSITY WITHIN THE TRADITION

Different denominations are called 'houses' or 'mansions' of Rastafari. Three of the oldest and most vital are the Twelve Tribes, Bobo Shanti, and therefore the Nyabinghi Order. The Twelve Tribes of Israel call themselves the 'real Jews' or Israelites and trace their descent to the twelve sons of Jacob. There are twelve denominations within the Twelve Tribes each named after one among the sons of Jacob, membership of every tribe depending on one's month of birth. they're more open to giving a role to women than some of the other mansions. Marley was a member of the Tribe of Joseph.

  The Nyabinghi Order (also referred to as the Nyabinghi House) takes its name from the East African resistance and spirit possession cult of the Kiga people against colonialism, which successively was named after a famous queen of the Kiga. The spirit of Nyabinghi was female and championed the explanation for the oppressed and exploited. The Nyabinghi Order was previously called Young Black Faith. It emerged within the late 1940s, founded by Arthur and Pan-Handle. it had been the Young

Black Faith who started wearing their hair in dreadlocks. They were more militant than the first Rastafari, taking their inspiration from the Mau Mau colonial resistance in Kenya. The Nyabinghi Order leadership is by elders and people who show the initiative and desire to lead; there is no formal structure for choosing elders beyond this form of self-selection.

The group founded by Prince Emmanuel Edwards are referred to as Bobo Shanti (or Bobo Ashanti, the Ethiopian National Congress, or Bobo Dread). Shanti refers to the Ashanti, the African tribe from which the bulk of Jamaicans are said to descend. they're one of the strictest Rastafari mansions, forming more of a proper church than the others. Prince Emmanuel is considered a God, a part of the trinity with Haile Selassie and Marcus Garvey. The Bobo ask him as 'dada'. The Bobo see themselves as a 'priestly order' of Rastas. they need a more formal church structure, with a selected church building, services from sundown Friday to sundown Saturday, and that they prostrate in silent prayer at meetings. They sleep in a self-sufficient commune on Bobo Hill outside southern magnolia in Jamaica. They wear their dreadlocks tightly wrapped in turbans and clothe themselves in priestly robes. After Prince Emmanuel's death, they split into three groups, all of which survive Bobo Hill.

Some Rastafari groups exclude White race , viewing them as having no authentic reference to Africa. However, in recent decades there are white Rastas, as parts of the movement have moved beyond black supremacy to seeing all races as Jah's children and therefore the unity of all people of the world.

ATTITUDES TO OTHER RELIGIONS AND INTERFAITH ACTIVITIES

Christianity is seen because the religion of the oppressors. Slaves in Jamaica were excluded from the Anglican Christianity practised by British colonials because it had been seen as too sophisticated for them and it was thought that they might be inspired to think of themselves as equals within the eyes of God. within the past Catholicism was also abhorred because of the link with Italy as the power invading what was then Abyssinia. Rastas were seen by Christians as outcasts in Jamaican society: as criminals, poor, and not respectable. This began to vary in the latter part of the 20th century, however, as Rastas lost a number of their outcast status.

   There are, moreover, several points of convergence between Rastas and Christians; both revere Christ, for instance . However, for Christians the veneration of Haile Selassie as the messiah is a heresy.

In the late 1990s some prominent Rastas converted to Evangelical Christianity. The Ethiopian Orthodox Church is an inspiration and influence because this was the religion of Haile Selassie. Marley was baptised into the Ethiopian Orthodox Church shortly before his death in 1980. There are few organised interfaith activities by Rastas inasmuch as there are few organised activities by Rastas. Members of other faiths are welcomed into ceremonies counting on the relationship with the specific group of Rastas holding the ceremony.

CHAPTER 5

MEANING AND PURPOSE

Rastas experience spiritual states through smoking ganja, drumming, and chanting. Religious experience may be a way of testing
whatever they hear to discern its truth. there's an avoidance of dogma and an emphasis on intelligence, as in reasoning sessions. Individual experience is central to the present . it's a rejection of the racist denigration of black intellect as inferior, and the
history of persecution in Jamaica during which authorities sentenced Rastafari to mental institutions for their beliefs. Rastafari

interpret world events during a religious framework, especially events concerning Africa.

ANSWERS TO ULTIMATE QUESTIONS

"There is nothing neither bad or good, but thinking makes it so" (Barrett 1977: 140). Early preachers focused on the identity of God. God as a Black African king undermined the status quo in colonialism and the Christian God. Rastafari 'test' what they hear and skim , discerning the reality to ultimate questions through intuition. they are doing this through 'head resting' with Jah, communicating on a private basis with divinity. it's also done collectively at reasoning sessions and Nyabinghi, during which they reflect on the Bible and history to come to an understanding. Truth is

grounded in 'dread' "the confrontation of nation with a primordial but historically denied racial selfhood" (Clarke 1986: 64). Rastafari are inspired and authenticated by the Bible, as they understand and interpret it. They use the Bible and also the 'book within', intuition and experience, which comes from inner divine presence. Personal experience is that the most valid way of establishing truth, a way of
listening to and being guided by Jah. Rastafari 'know' Jah; they are doing not just put faith in him. Knowing Jah means knowing oneself because the inner self is divine. it's not a question of belief but of knowledge, which for the Rastafari means being within the
position of the master instead of the slave. They know their destiny and purpose, they determine events, and that they are not

determined by them. Knowing history and predicting the longer term through knowing Jah suggests the importance of memory in constituting life for the Rastafari. Science is seen as Babylon's tool. it's part of technocratic imperialism. Rastafari attempt to turn away from the materialism, mass media, and commodity fetishism of white European supremacy. there's an antipathy to white man's ideas. When the sociologist Leonard E. Barrett attended a Nyabinghi, he was accosted for carrying cameras and tape machine , which were called the tools of Babylon. Rastafari prefer natural things, living 'naturally', which suggests in accordance with their interpretation of 'the laws of nature'. this will mean that Rastafari can be sceptical of some forms of biomedicine, like vaccinations.

Science and technology are seen as artificial and unnatural. they create evil things like weapons of mass destruction. They are a means of enslaving man to machine, in order that he is unable to do things for himself, like Africans were once they were used as
slaves.

CHAPTER 6

VALUES AND COMMITMENT

Understanding how moral values and a way of obligation can come from beliefs and experience;
Evaluating their own and others' values so as to make informed, rational and imaginative choices.

MORAL ISSUES

Rastafari oppose abortion and contraception, which they see as a colonial strategy to suppress the African population. Some Rastafari women do still use contraception,

however. Medicines are often a problem,
Rastafari don't use patent medicines,
instead they use herbal remedies from folk
traditions if they will . Consumerism
dominates Babylon, so Rastafari shy away
from materialist consumerist things and
check out to live 'naturally'. They reject
consumerism and materialism as colonialist
wastefulness.
Entrepreneurial activity may be a way to
independence from the colonial system.
they like self-employment to dependence on
wage labour whether or not the income is
lower, because wage labour is seen as a sort
of slaver.

ETHICAL GUIDELINES

Marijuana has been smoked since the time
of the top commune in the 1940s. the

precise form of marijuana smoked is known as 'ganja' in Jamaica. it's a sacrament for the Rastafari. it had been seen as a way of opposing colonial society and asserting their own authentic sort of freedom. Since it's illegal in Jamaica, smoking ganja may be a way of showing freedom from the laws of Babylon, although recently it had been decriminalised in small amounts for religious use by practising adult Rastafari. Furthermore, it is believed that ganja enhances spiritual states and reduces stress, produces visions, brings unity and communal feelings, and
bestows tranquillity to the dispossessed. Ganja has become a dominant symbol of the Rastafari, who call it 'callie' and 'iley'. Ganja is seen as a natural product or herb, not as a drug. For the Rastafari, the free smoking of ganja may be a religious right

and an issue of spiritual freedom; however it is seen as criminal activity by most governments. one among the reasons Rastafari in the 20th century were related to criminality by authorities is their connection with growing and distributing marijuana. Rastafari have a strict diet called Ital, or 'natural' food, which suggests the essence of things or things in their natural states. Ital refers to "a complex of lifeways that provide an alternative to the unnatural man-made Babylon system" (Christensen 2014: 142).

The Ital complex came from the I-gelic House mansion who lived within the hills beyond the Kingston ghetto in the mid-1950s to mid-1960s. Ital food is usually fruit and vegetables, grown without fertilisers. Rastafari aren't allowed to consume alcohol, milk, coffee, salt, oil , cigarettes, heroin, or cocaine. Vegetarianism is preferred, but those that do eat meat avoid pork, shellfish, scaleless fish or snails, and fish over 12 inches long. this is often similar to the Jewish Kosher diet, and Rastafaris are following the identical Leviticus dietary and hygiene rules. Additionally, pig and cod are related to slave food. Pigs are taboo animals. Rastafari prefer food from their own plantations and avoid food from unknown sources. They follow the principle of

naturalism in care as well, washing hair with only water and locally grown herbs. They avoid chemically processed goods, they are doing not use soap or shampoo. Dreadlocks form when hair is left alone and unbrushed, but some do comb and groom them. Herbs and things from the world are good. They also follow Old Testament prohibitions on trimming or shaving the hair, tattoos, and cutting flesh in any way, as mentioned above. Women don't wear makeup, use hair chemicals, or wear immodest clothes. Some women observe menstrual taboos and can't cook for their husbands while menstruating. Rastafari reject war because the destructive practice of Babylon and tend to be pacifists.

INDIVIDUAL RESPONSIBILITY

There is a dominance of individualism among Rastafari. 'I and I' may be a philosophy of radical individualism. Jah dwells within each person. everyone is held responsible for him or herself as an outcome of the belief that each person is an incarnation of Jah, the divine, which suggests each. this suggests their practices have a freedom of association and participation. There are not any institutional commitments required for Rastafari. Being Rastafari comes from individual conviction. Most Rastafari aren't affiliated with institutional forms like Bobo Shanti or the Twelve Tribes. they're an atomised population with no network of structured contact. they like self-reliance to handouts. Individual autonomy is especially important as part of rejecting the legacy of slavery.

The individualism of Rastafari is balanced by an ethic of unity. this is often a way of bringing Rastas together for communal purposes. All black people are thought to descend from common ancestors in Africa that were separated by slavery. Rastas act as self-conscious members of a brotherhood and sisterhood, sharing with one another , especially amongst the poor. They call each other 'brethren' and 'sistren' to emphasise spiritual kinship. They emphasise the kinship of humanity under the fatherhood of Jah. Spiritual brotherhood doesn't necessarily mean racial exclusivity, however, although black supremacy is a facet of the Rastafari movement. Rastas as brethren attempt to work together to harness individual spiritual power and create a positive, life affirming philosophy for self and community. a method this is done is through one-to-one teaching by brethren and sistren,summed up within the phrase "each one teach one". State education is seen as indoctrination within the colonial or post-colonial system, called 'head-decay-shun'. Camps and yards are centers of learning the Rastafari way of seeing the planet .

Rastafari endeavour to measure in harmony with nature, as a part of the oneness with Jah. 'Mother Nature' or 'Mother Earth' is divine and to be revered as Jah's creation. 'Sitting within the dust' means remaining close to earth, the first manifestation of nature and developing an understanding of the way to live in harmony with nature's laws. Babylon destroys Mother Earth, by making weapons, especially nuclear weapons, to destroy everything.

GLOBAL VISION

Rastafari has extended beyond Jamaica, to the united kingdom and USA in particular. There also are smaller Rasta populations in Japan, New Zealand, Brazil, and other countries. Some Rastas haven't any ethnic

link at all with Afro-Caribbean people; not only are there
white Rastas but also Rastas of Native American background, and Japanese background, among others. Rastafari spread internationally through the migration of Jamaicans and therefore the popularity of reggae music. Rastafari symbols of colour, hair, language, and Ital diet became symbols of identity for Jamaican and non-Jamaican youth more generally. Rastafari symbols became related to gang violence in Jamaica and then the drug trade in cocaine with US. However, those that
adopted the symbols often didn't also have the religious values of the Rastafari. This, alongside the sacramental use of ganja, associated Rastafaris with drugs and as addicts within the US, which many

Rastafari felt was an unfair and inaccurate association.

  In the UK, Rastafari was haunted by second-generation immigrants from Jamaica and the Caribbean from the 1970s onwards. It has become more common since then for young people in particular to dress as Rastas without following the religious values.

WEBSITES

Information on Haile Selassie's home during his exile in Bath, UK: www.fairfieldhousebath.org Article on Haile Selassie's exile in the UK: https://discoversociety.org/2014/07/01/focus-when-britain-loved-rastafari/ 'Jamaican Religions' on The Pluralism Project: http://pluralism.org/religions/afro-caribbean/afro-caribbean-traditions/jamaicanreligion/ 'Rastafari' on BBC Religion: http://www.bbc.co.uk/religion/religions/rastafari/ 'What Do Rastafarians Believe' on Jamaicans.com: http://jamaicans.com/believe/ 'Rastafari' on Wikipedia: https://en.wikipedia.org/wiki/Rastafari 'Understanding Rastafari' on the Jamaica Gleaner: http://jamaica-gleaner.com/article/news/20150509/understa nding-rastafaripart-ii Article on Rasta community in Shashamane, Ethiopia: http://www.bbc.co.uk/news/magazine-28059303

BIBLIOGRAPHY

BARNETT, M (ED.) (2012) RASTAFARI IN THE NEW MILLENNIUM: A RASTAFARI READER. SYRACUSE: SYRACUSE UNIVERSITY PRESS. BARRETT, L. E. (1977) THE RASTAFARIANS: THE DREADLOCKS OF JAMAICA. LONDON: HEINEMANN. CAMPBELL, H. (1985) RASTA AND RESISTANCE: FROM MARCUS GARVEY TO WALTER RODNEY. LONDON: HANSIB PUBLISHING. CASHMORE, E. E. (1979) RASTAMAN: THE RASTAFARIAN MOVEMENT IN ENGLAND. LONDON: UNWIN PAPERBACKS. – (1984) THE RASTAFARIANS. LONDON: MINORITY RIGHTS GROUP. CHEVANNES, B. (1991)

'THE RASTAFARI OF JAMAICA', IN MILLER, T. (ED.) WHEN PROPHETS DIE: THE POSTCHARISMATIC FATE OF NEW RELIGIOUS MOVEMENTS. ALBANY: STATE UNIVERSITY OF NEW YORK PRESS. – (1994) RASTAFARI: ROOTS AND IDEOLOGY. SYRACUSE: SYRACUSE UNIVERSITY PRESS. – (1998A) 'INTRODUCING THE NATIVE RELIGIONS OF JAMAICA', IN CHEVANNES, B. (ED.) RASTAFARI AND OTHER AFRICAN-CARIBBEAN WORLDVIEWS. BASINGSTOKE AND LONDON: MACMILLAN, PP. 1-19. – (1998B) 'NEW APPROACH TO RASTAFARI', IN CHEVANNES, B. (ED.) RASTAFARI AND OTHER AFRICAN-CARIBBEAN WORLDVIEWS. BASINGSTOKE AND LONDON: MACMILLAN, PP. 20-42. CHRISTENSEN,

J. (2014) RASTAFARI REASONING AND THE RASTAWOMAN: GENDER CONSTRUCTIONS IN THE SHAPING OF RASTAFARI LIVITY. LANHAM: LEXINGTON BOOKS. CLARKE, P. B. (1986) BLACK PARADISE: THE RASTAFARIAN MOVEMENT. WELLINGBOROUGH: AQUARIAN PRESS. EDMONDS, E. B. (2003) RASTAFARI: FROM OUTCASTS TO CULTURE BEARERS. OXFORD: OXFORD UNIVERSITY PRESS. GARVEY, M. (1967) PHILOSOPHY AND OPINIONS. 3 VOLS. LONDON: CASS. HALL, S. (1985) 'RELIGIOUS IDEOLOGIES AND SOCIAL MOVEMENTS IN JAMAICA', IN BOCOCK, R. AND THOMPSON, K. (EDS.). RELIGION AND IDEOLOGY: A READER. MANCHESTER:

MANCHESTER UNIVERSITY PRESS, PP.
269-**296.**

9 7 9 8 8 4 5 8 5 8 3 7 5